PORTRAIT OF THE CANADIAN ROCKIES

PUBLISHED BY BELA BALIKO PHOTOGRAPHY, ALBERTA, CANADA

Published with pride in Alberta, Canada by

Bela Baliko Photography and Publishing Inc
Unit 1, 108 Boulder Crescent
Canmore, Alberta, Canada T1W 1L2
Tel: (403) 678-2010
Fax: (403) 678-2087

Website: www.belabaliko.com
E-mail: info@belabaliko.com

Editing, Layout and Design: Bela Baliko
Research and Editing: Susan Louise Baliko
Author's Biography and Portrait: Susan Louise Baliko
Printed in Calgary, Alberta by Quebecor World Calgary

Third Printing 2001
ISBN 1-894729-00-5
Previously listed as ISBN 0-921146-01-9

Front Cover: Mount Rundle
Page 1: Bighorn Sheep Ewe
Page 3: Indian Paintbrush
Page 5: Pika
Page 7: Mount Assiniboine
Back Cover: Prairie Crocus

For my wife, Susan.

For all her patience, love and friendship.

For believing in and sharing my dream.

INTRODUCTION

Portrait *noun.* *1.* A likeness, especially of the face, produced, usually from life, by an artist or photographer. *2.* A vivid word description, portrayal, etc.

Canadian Rockies *noun.* *1.* Chain of mountains found in Western Canada covering an area of approximately 155,000 square kilometres (60,000 sq mi). *2.* One of the last great areas of wilderness in North America.

Portrait of the Canadian Rockies *book.* *1.* An intimate portrayal of the rugged wilderness known as the Canadian Rockies. *2.* A close-up look at the flora and fauna which inhabit this region.

The Canadian Rockies are unique and for the most part an unpopulated and unspoiled wilderness, from the massive Columbia Icefield whose meltwater feeds three of the world's great oceans, to the delicate beauty of the tiny Alpine Forget-Me-Not. The camera is the ideal tool for recording these marvellous wonders as it preserves the moment, leaving the subjects untouched. This is also the intent of *"Portrait of the Canadian Rockies"*, to portray the grandeur of this pristine wilderness. It is a book for all who love and respect these magnificent mountains and wish to preserve them.

ALPINE FORGET-ME-NOT
Myosotis alpestris

This beautiful little perennial renowned for its vivid colour and exquisite fragrance is the official state flower of Alaska. It blooms from mid-June to mid-August and can be found throughout the Canadian Rockies growing in moist open subalpine and alpine meadows at elevations above 1,370 metres (4,500 ft). The Alpine Forget-Me-Not is a member of the Borage family along with the Stickseed, Clustered Oreocarya and the Stoneseed. It is often mistaken for the Alpine Speedwell *(Veronica wormskjoldii)* since the colour, size and height of the flowers are similar.

The plant begins with furry lance-shaped leaves approximately 2.5 cm (1 in) in length. These are followed by the first tiny blooms measuring only .5 cm (3/16 in) in width. The flowers have five petals which are sky-blue in colour. Upon opening, the star-shaped centre of the bloom is often pink, changing to a bright yellow colour. These first flowers blossom on short stems close to the ground. The stems continue to grow, lifting the cluster of flowers up to 20 cm (8 in) in height. Each plant has several stems topped by a collection of blooms. After the flower fades four tiny nut-like pods remain which contain the seeds.

PEYTO LAKE
Banff National Park

This magnificent lake fed by the Peyto Glacier, part of the Wapta Icefield, is located 40 kilometres (25 mi) north of Lake Louise on the Icefields Parkway. The lake was named after English born Ebenezer William Peyto (1868-1943) by American writer and explorer Walter Dwight Wilcox (1869-1949). Wilcox greatly admired "Wild" Bill as a guide, outfitter and mountain man and after having travelled hundreds of miles together, considered Peyto to be the best in the Rockies. Peyto was the guide for many famous people of the day including Edward Whymper (1840-1910), the British mountaineer who was the first to conquer the Matterhorn in 1865.

After serving in the Boer War (1899-1902), "Wild" Bill came west to work for the Canadian Pacific Railway and stayed on to become a trapper, prospector, guide and outfitter, specializing in taking adventurous tourists into the wilds of the Canadian Rocky Mountains on horseback. Peyto was known for his dependability, honesty, knowledge of the area and his eccentricity. Always wearing a white scarf, fringed buckskin jacket, wide-brimmed sombrero and well-worn pants he was without question the most colourful figure in Banff. In 1911 Peyto became a warden with the Rocky Mountains Park later known as Banff National Park and headquartered at Healy Creek until his retirement in 1936.

MOUNTAIN GOAT
Oreamnos americanus

The Mountain Goat is actually a type of mountain antelope. They are seldom seen since goats prefer rugged rocky terrain above 2,000 metres (6,500 ft). Ideally suited for this harsh and unforgiving environment, these animals have a thick shaggy coat which has 15 to 20 cm (6 to 8 in) long guard hairs with a 10 cm (4 in) inner layer of wool to keep them warm. Their hooves, split, sharp-edged, flexible and rubbery, enable them to climb effortlessly along sheer rock faces even when covered with snow or ice. Due to this agility mountain goats have few natural enemies.

Goats eat a wide variety of vegetation allowing them to live year round at higher elevations, but do travel to mineral licks found in the valleys in the spring and summer. Distinguishing the sex of a goat is difficult because of their long coats and both the males and females carry short, black, dagger-like horns. The males or billies are slightly larger with longer and more curved horns and are generally solitary animals, never seen with kids. Females or nannies give birth to one or occasionally two kids each year usually in the month of May and often group together during the summer months. Mountain goats live to be 10 to 15 years old.

MOUNT RUNDLE
Banff National Park

At 22 kilometres (14 mi) in length, with the Banff townsite at its base, Mount Rundle is perhaps the most recognized landmark in the Canadian Rockies. The 2,949 metre (9,675 ft) peak was named after Robert Terrill Rundle (1811-1896), a Methodist missionary who ministered to the Indians of the region during the 1840's. Sir James Hector (1834-1907) named the mountain in honour of Reverend Rundle in 1858. Hector was the surgeon and geologist of the Palliser Expedition (1857-1860), led by John Palliser (1807-1887), which explored and surveyed much of western British North America.

Robert Terrill Rundle came to Banff from his native England in 1840 as a guest of the Canadian Pacific Railway. He was the first missionary to the Indians of the area and was very highly regarded by them. Rundle learned to speak and write fluently in Cree, the language of the Stoneys. He held many open-air services for them in the meadows at the foot of the mountain which now bears his name and on the shore of Lake Minnewanka. Reverend Rundle lived among the Stoney Indians for eight years while he ministered to them but was forced to return to England due to ill health in 1848.

PIKA
Ochotona princeps

The proper pronunciation is "peek-a" not "pie-ka". This small mammal, 15 cm (6 in) in length and weighing only 140 g (5 oz), is a member of the Lagomorph family, the same family as rabbits and hares and is also appropriately known as the "Rock Rabbit". It can be found throughout the Rockies living on rock slides and talus slopes from elevations of 1,800 to 2,600 metres (6,000 to 8,500 ft). The Pika's colour varies from grey to reddish brown depending on the colour of the rocks it inhabits, giving it near perfect camouflage. If it moves to a new area its colour will gradually change to match its new surroundings.

The Pika does not hibernate, so it spends its time collecting vegetation throughout the summer, spreading it out on the rocks to dry for the winter. One Pika may hoard as much as 23 kg (50.5 lbs), or 150 times its own body weight, to feed on during the long alpine winter. Perfectly suited to remain active throughout the winter, the little Pika has insulating fur and fur-soled feet which enable it to run over and under the snow in complete comfort. In May, when fresh vegetation is plentiful, the Pika breeds and gives birth to three or four offspring.

PRAIRIE CROCUS
Anemone patens

This delicate flower is the floral emblem of Manitoba and the state flower of South Dakota. The Prairie Crocus, also known as the "Wild Crocus" and the "Pasque Flower" since it blossoms at Easter, is one of the first alpine blooms of spring. This perennial grows on open dry hillsides and forest clearings on south-facing slopes. It occurs throughout the Canadian Rockies at all elevations below the timberline, lower than 2,450 metres (8,000 ft). This member of the Buttercup Family can be seen in April and early May. Beautiful blooms of purple, mauve, lavender and occasionally white often emerge through the snow before it melts.

The buds are followed by furry immature purplish leaves. The stem, the leaves and the petal-like sepals are covered with fine hairs to insulate the plant from the cold. The six-sepalled flower opens up in full sunlight measuring up to 7.5 cm (3 in) in width then closes again overnight enveloping the bright yellow stamens within. After the bloom has matured, the stem lengthens to about 20 cm (8 in) and the lacy leaves develop fully becoming green and delicate. The showy sepals are replaced in early summer by a head of silky grey styles about 2.5 cm (1 in) in length, each attached to a seed.

CASTLE MOUNTAIN
Banff National Park

Sir James Hector (1834-1907), surgeon and geologist of the Palliser Expedition (1857-1860), first sighted this impressive mountain in 1858. Noting its distinctive appearance he appropriately christened it Castle Mountain. The name stood until 1946 when it was changed to Mount Eisenhower by Canadian Prime Minister William Lyon Mackenzie King (1874-1950) in honour of General Dwight D. Eisenhower (1890-1969), Supreme Commander of the Allied Forces in World War II. In 1979 "Castle Mountain" was officially reinstated, as both Canadians and Americans resented the replacing of such an appropriate and long-standing title. However, the southeast tower of this mountain still bears Eisenhower's name.

Located 30 kilometres (19 mi) northwest of the Banff townsite and standing at an elevation of 2,766 metres (9,075 ft), Castle Mountain is an excellent example of a "castellate" peak. These mountains are common throughout the main ranges, which rise approximately 500 metres (1,640 ft) higher than the peaks of the front ranges. Castellate mountains are similar to "fault thrust" mountains like Mount Rundle, except that the underlying soft layers of shale on the smooth sloped side were eroded away, in this case by the Bow River. This erosion caused the top harder layers of limestone and dolomite to break off, leaving the sheer precipices of today.

COMMON LOON
Gavia immer

The Common Loon, one of four species that can be found in the Canadian Rockies, is the only species which breeds here. These striking birds can be seen on montane and lower subalpine lakes up to an elevation of 2,150 metres (7,000 ft). Only one pair of birds will be seen on a lake as they are very territorial. The same pair uses the nesting site year after year for as long as the birds are together. Two eggs are laid, with usually only one hatching in mid-June. Immediately after hatching, loon chicks leave the nest and begin swimming with their parents.

The loon has a wing span of 1.5 metres (5 ft). Their wings are proportionately shorter, narrower and more pointed than that of most birds. They have heavy sharp-edged bills and their bodies are long and heavy due to their solid bone structure. The legs are short with webbed feet and are positioned far back on its body. These characteristics are ideally suited for diving and swimming, a necessity as their diet consists mainly of fish. Loons can dive to depths of over 100 metres (300 ft) for up to three minutes and are excellent swimmers, using their wings as well as their feet.

MORAINE LAKE
Banff National Park

Moraine Lake, located 16 kilometres (10 mi) south of the village of Lake Louise, was named by Walter Dwight Wilcox (1869-1949), a Yale graduate who came to the area in 1893 with four of his classmates to explore, map, photograph and survey this newly accessible wilderness. Returning to Lake Louise almost every year of his life thereafter, he found Moraine Lake in 1899 while exploring the valley with Yale colleague, Samuel Evans Stokes Allen (1874-1945). Wilcox thought the lake was formed by blockage from a glacial moraine and so it was named. He published two books popularizing the area which significantly increased the flood of tourists and adventurers.

The valley enclosing the lake is known as the Valley of the Ten Peaks, or the Wenkchemna Peaks. Allen, a linguistic scholar, named them using the Stoney Indian words for the numbers one through ten, "Wenkchemna" meaning ten. Three peaks still retain their original Stoney names but the others were renamed. Peak six was renamed Mount Allen in 1898 by Wilcox. Allen suffered from severe depression brought about by his parents' strong disapproval of his active interest in the Canadian Rockies. After several further trips to the mountains with Wilcox, Samuel Allen was committed to a psychiatric hospital in 1905 where he spent the rest of his life.

WAPITI (ELK)
Cervus elaphus

Early explorers and travellers called them "red deer". Today they are known as "elk" but the official Canadian name for the second largest member of the deer family is the Wapiti, a Shawnee Indian word meaning "white rump". Males (bulls) can weigh up to 450 kg (990 lbs) and sport a rack measuring 1.2 to 1.5 metres (4 to 5 ft) in length and weighing 20 kg (44 lbs). The racks are shed in early spring and by the end of August the new set is fully grown. The velvet is rubbed off and the points are polished on trees and shrubs in preparation for the annual rut.

The rut starts early in September and continues throughout the month of October. The males bugle loudly from dusk to dawn to attract females (cows) and form harems. "Fencing" matches occur when bulls defend their harems, locking antlers together and violently pushing and shoving one another back and forth until one forces the other's head down. Harems of up to 80 cows are not un-common. Females weigh about 225 kg (495 lbs) and give birth to spotted calves, occasionally twins, in late May and into the month of June. The calves stay with the cows for two years and reach full maturity in three years.

LAKE LOUISE
Banff National Park

Lake Louise, known to the Stoney Indians as "The Lake of the Little Fishes", was first visited by guide and outfitter Tom Wilson (1859-1933) and an Indian guide, Edwin Hunter, in 1882. Wilson named it "Emerald Lake" and so it was known until it was renamed by the Canadian Pacific Railway (CPR) after Queen Victoria's fourth daughter, Princess Louise Caroline Alberta (1848-1939). Princess Louise was married to the Marquis of Lorne, Governor General of Canada from 1878 to 1883. Neither Princess Louise nor Queen Victoria ever visited the lake. In the 1890's Lake Louise became a major destination for mountaineers from America, England and Europe.

The peaks seen in this photograph from left to right are: Mount Lefroy, elevation 3,423 metres (11,230 ft), named after Captain John Henry Lefroy (1817-1890), Director of the Magnetic Survey of Canada. Mount Victoria, elevation 3,464 metres (11,365 ft) and the Victoria Glacier, named in honour of HRH Queen Victoria (1819-1901). Mount Whyte, elevation 2,983 metres (9,787 ft), named for Sir William Whyte (1843-1914), Vice-President of the CPR. The Beehive, elevation 2,274 metres (7,460 ft), so named due to its shape by Samuel Evans Stokes Allen (1874-1945). Mount Niblock, elevation 2,976 metres (9,764 ft) named after John Niblock (1849-1914), Western Superintendent of the CPR.

CLARK'S NUTCRACKER
Nucifraga columbiana

The Clark's Nutcracker was named after American explorer, Captain William Clark (1770-1838) of the Lewis and Clark Expedition (1804-1806). The expedition was sent to map and explore new American territory west of the Mississippi River and to catalogue plant and animal life. This member of the crow family, measuring 32 cm (13 in) in length, is a year-round resident of the southern and central Canadian Rocky Mountains and lives in subalpine forests below the timberline generally ranging from 2,150 to 2,450 metres (7,000 to 8,000 ft). Nutcrackers have a unique swooping style of flight and often free-fall from great heights before suddenly opening their wings to alight on a branch.

The Nutcracker is appropriately named as it uses its large powerful bill to "hammer" and crack open conifer cones and extract the seeds, their main food source. Nutcrackers will also eat berries and insects. These birds are very intelligent and will stockpile food in as many as 2,000 different locations, managing to remember where most of their caches are hidden. These stashes of food see the Nutcracker through the long alpine winter until new food sources become available. In February, they build nests in coniferous trees like the Engelmann Spruce, Whitebark Pine or the Subalpine Fir. Two to three eggs are laid each year.

YELLOW CLEMATIS
Clematis tangutica

The Yellow Clematis like the Blue Clematis *(Clematis columbiana)* escaped cultivation and can be found scattered throughout the lower montane regions of the Rocky Mountains. Growing on talus slopes, in clearings and at the edge of deciduous woods, this trailing vine is found around the base of trees, climbing on bushes and shrubs or in clumps in open areas. This beautiful flower is a member of the Buttercup family, a very diverse family which includes the Prairie Crocus, the Mountain Marsh Marigold, Columbines, Anemones, Baneberry and the Buttercups. The only native Clematis occurring in the Canadian Rockies is the Western Clematis *(Clematis ligusticifolia)*.

The Yellow Clematis blooms during the months of June and July and is very similar to the Blue Clematis in appearance, except for its colour. The bloom is 5 to 10 cm (2 to 4 in) in width and is composed of four petal-like sepals in bright yellow with a cluster of stamens in the centre. The flower hangs down from a short stem branching off the vine which has shiny dark green leaves growing in sets of five. The bloom fades in August and is replaced by a woolly "mop" of styles approximately 5 cm (2 in) in length with seeds attached. These styles remain on the plant well into September until they are scattered by the wind. The vine overwinters and revives again in the spring.

33

MOUNT ASSINIBOINE
Mount Assiniboine Provincial Park

Long before the arrival of the explorers and fur traders, the Assiniboine Indians ventured far into the mountains to hunt on the plateau beneath this towering pyramid. Mount Assiniboine was named in their honour by George Mercer Dawson (1849-1901), geologist and Director of the Geological Survey of Canada. Dawson was conducting a topographical survey of the Canadian Rocky Mountains from 1881 to 1884 when he came across this spectacular peak. Sir James Outram (1864-1925), a British alpinist who emigrated to Victoria, British Columbia, in 1900, made the first official ascent of Mount Assiniboine in 1901.

Also known as the "Matterhorn of the Rockies", this prominent peak is located on the border of Banff National Park and Mount Assiniboine Provincial Park in British Columbia, which was established on February 6, 1922 at the urging of the Alpine Club of Canada. The park is only accessible by helicopter or on foot with the shortest and most direct route 27 kilometres (17 mi) in length via the Mount Shark and Bryant Creek trails to Assiniboine Pass. Mount Assiniboine, surrounded by Mount Magog, Lunette Peak, Mount Sturdee and The Marshall, each exceeding 3,100 metres (10,000 ft), is the highest peak in the southern Canadian Rockies standing at an elevation of 3,618 metres (11,870 ft).

35

BIGHORN SHEEP
Ovis canadensis

Rocky Mountain Bighorn Sheep have long been a symbol of the mountains and the high country. A fully mature ram can weigh 160 kg (350 lbs) with a pair of magnificent horns measuring up to 1.3 metres (4 ft 4 in) in length. Their lives are spent grazing and relaxing, laying around storing energy for the long winter and chewing their cud. Bighorns migrate seasonally from the grassy slopes found in the valleys to alpine meadows in the high country. They always graze near a rock out-cropping or ledge in order to have an escape route from predators like the grizzly bear, cougar and wolf.

November signifies the start of the annual rut for the Bighorn Sheep. Rams of similar stature and horn size will challenge each other to head-butting duels for the right to breed with the ewes. First the rams tilt their heads to show each other the size of their curl. If the challenge continues, both opponents rear up on their hind legs, take a few steps and fall forward crashing their horns together until the weaker animal gives up. The seriousness of these autumn matches leaves many contestants with broken and splintered horns. Sounds of butting horns echo throughout the mountains and can be heard as far as a kilometre away.

TAKAKKAW FALLS
Yoho National Park

Sir William Cornelius Van Horne (1843-1915), General Manager of the Canadian Pacific Railway from 1882 to 1899, saw this awe-inspiring 380 metre (1,247 ft) waterfall, located 40 kilometres (25 mi) west of the village of Lake Louise, in 1897 while inspecting the rail line across the Canadian Rockies. He named the falls "Takakkaw", the Stoney Indian word for "it is magnificent". Takakkaw is fed by meltwater from the massive Daly Glacier, named after Joseph Francis Daly (1840-1916), Past-President of the American Geographical Society. The Daly Glacier is part of the great Waputik Icefield located north of the falls.

The incredible beauty of Takakkaw and the surrounding area were first brought to the government's attention by Dr. Jean Habel (1839-1902), a German scientist and alpinist who came to explore the Yoho valley and nearby Mount des Poilus, elevation 3,161 metres (10,370 ft). Habel came through the Yoho Pass to the previously inaccessible valley and was astounded by the savage force of the falls and the grandeur of its setting. In 1901 the area was designated as "park reserve" to preserve the wonders of Yoho. Under the Dominion Forest Reserves and Parks Act, the park reserve became Yoho National Park in 1911.

COLUMBIAN GROUND SQUIRREL

Spermophilus columbianus

The Columbian Ground Squirrel inhabits fields and forest clearings throughout the Canadian Rockies, from valley floors to high alpine meadows ranging from 1,370 to 2,450 metres (4,500 to 8,000 ft) in elevation. This "fair-weather" rodent measuring 15 to 20 cm (6 to 8 in) in length with a 7.5 cm (3 in) tail and weighing between 455 to 950 g (1 to 2 lbs) spends most of its life underground. From late April to late August when the weather is the mildest they are totally occupied with eating seeds, berries, leaves, stems and roots, building up fat reserves to see them through eight months of hibernation.

Columbian Ground Squirrels live in large colonies in maze-like burrows with an average of ten entrances. One squirrel acts as a sentry while the others play and forage for food. At the first sign of danger the lookout "peeps" loudly, warning the other members of the colony to retreat to the safety of their dens. However, predators like the grizzly bear and the badger are very capable of digging them out, especially since the squirrels often burrow into loose sandy soil. Mating occurs usually in May when the males fight one another for the right to breed with the females. About three weeks later the females give birth to two to seven offspring.

THE THREE SISTERS
Kananaskis Country

In 1883 these prominent peaks were known as "The Three Nuns" and provided the backdrop for the small mining community of Canmore, seven kilometres (4.3 mi) to the north, nestled in the Bow Valley. George Mercer Dawson (1849-1901), Director of the Geographical Survey of Canada, renamed this magnificent mountain "The Three Sisters" out of respect for Reverend Robert Terrill Rundle (1811-1896), a Methodist missionary to the Indians of the area during the 1840's, as this was a more appropriate Protestant designation. Story has it that each peak carried the name of one of Reverend Rundle's three sisters. Unofficially the peaks are locally known as Faith, Hope and Charity.

The former Canadian Pacific Railway employees who discovered the hot springs in Banff in 1883, Frank McCabe and the two McCardell brothers, William and Tom, found a coal seam while prospecting just west of the Three Sisters in 1884. In 1886 HRH Queen Victoria (1819-1901) granted a charter to allow coal mining in Canmore. The "Number One Mine" was opened in 1887. It proved to be the best-producing mine of those that were worked in the Bow Valley and remained in operation until its closure in 1979. In 1921, M.B. Morrow, General Manager of the Canmore Coal Company, made the first official ascent of the peaks, climbing the middle Sister at 2,769 metres (9,085 ft).

MULE DEER
Odocoileus hemionus

The most common deer found in the Rocky Mountains is the Mule Deer so named because of their large mule-like ears. In early spring the males (bucks) shed their antlers. Old antlers are an important source of food and minerals for many rodents like the porcupine. New antlers begin as buds and by the end of August have reached their full size. Antlers are bony outgrowths of the skull which grow rapidly, nourished by a furry outer skin called "velvet" that is rich with blood. Once growth is complete, the velvet dries out. The buck rubs the velvet off, polishes the points and is ready for the annual rut.

Females (does) give birth to one or two fawns usually in the month of June. They are able to stand almost immediately after birth. For the first few weeks, the fawns have no odour and are able to lay down undetected in the grass while the doe grazes nearby. She comes back often to nurse the fawn, clean its coat and ingest its waste. Fawns stay with the doe for approximately two years and then generally form into small herds around an older doe. Bucks tend to be solitary during the rut, but are commonly seen in groups of two to five throughout the summer.

PAINTBRUSH
Castilleja rhexifolia

This member of the Figwort family is one of the most abundant and colourful flowers in the Canadian Rockies. The Paintbrush blooms from June to September and can be found at all elevations from valley floor to timberline, growing mainly in meadows and open woods. This semi-parasitic plant is usually found in large clumps. The roots of the Paintbrush invade and steal nourishment from the roots of neighbouring plants. Its related species grow from 10 to 60 cm (4 to 24 in) in height with lightly-haired leaves and stems. The vibrant colours of the Paintbrush are not flowers but are actually modified leaves called "bracts". The true flower is the light green tube in the centre of each bract.

Only a few species of paintbrush are clearly identifiable. There are many natural hybrids between species that share different characteristics of each parent plant, producing wide colour shifts within species. At lower elevations the Common Red Paintbrush is most abundant but it also includes colour variations from pale orange to deep crimson and grows to be 60 cm (24 in) in height. At subalpine elevations the Rosy Paintbrush has frilly blooms varying from dark pink to white, only growing to 10 cm (4 in) in height. Other varieties of paintbrush feature yellow, purple or cream-coloured blooms.

ATHABASCA GLACIER
Jasper National Park

In 1898 two mountain climbers from England, John Norman Collie (1859-1942) and Herman Woolley (1846-1920), made the first official ascent of Mount Athabasca. From the 3,491 metre (11,453 ft) summit, Collie and Woolley discovered the Columbia Icefield, the largest of seventeen named icefields located along the Continental Divide. Covering an area of 325 square kilometres (125 sq mi), the Columbia Icefield is the largest permanent body of ice and snow south of the Arctic Circle and is also the hydrographic apex of North America. Meltwater from the Icefield drains into the Pacific, Arctic and Atlantic Oceans.

The Athabasca Glacier is one of eight large glaciers fed by the Columbia Icefield. Located 95 kilometres (59 mi) south of Jasper and reaching to within one kilometre (.5 mi) of Highway 93, the Athabasca is the most accessible glacier along the Icefields Parkway. Flowing over a series of icefalls below the Columbia Icefield, the massive Athabasca Glacier extends six kilometres (3.75 mi) in length and one kilometre (.5 mi) in width and consists of solid ice that is over 300 metres (1,000 ft) thick. Currently the Athabasca Glacier is receding but other glaciers in the area like the Saskatchewan Glacier are advancing.

HOARY MARMOT
Marmota caligata

This large rodent is actually a member of the Squirrel family, a surprising fact considering that adults may weigh 9 kg (20 lbs). The word "hoary" refers to the Marmot's grey–tipped outer guard hairs which cover a coarse thick coat of brown fur. They are also appropriately known as "Whistlers" because of their shrill one–note warning call, used to alert other members of their group when predators like the grizzly bear approach. These very social animals can be found in groups of up to 20 members and prefer to live on rocky slopes at elevations of 2,075 to 2,450 metres (6,800 to 8,000 ft).

Marmots build an extensive network of underground tunnels which lead to warm grass–lined dens deep within the loose rock. These dens protect the Marmots from predators and the bitterly cold harsh winters of their subalpine habitat during hibernation. In April or May they awaken from their long deep sleep and spend the summer months dining on a variety of tundra vegetation, sunning themselves on rocks and building up layers of body fat. They breed and return to their dens to bed down for the winter in September. The females mate every second year and give birth to two to five offspring during the month of June.

MOUNT ANDROMEDA
Jasper National Park

Located 129 kilometres (80 mi) north of Lake Louise on the Icefields Parkway and standing at an elevation of 3,450 metres (11,319 ft), Mount Andromeda cradles a portion of the massive Columbia Icefield and towers over the giant Athabasca Glacier which slowly flows past its base. This magnificent three peaked summit was named in 1938 by Major Edwin Rex Gibson (1892-1957), Past-President of the Alpine Club of Canada, after the wife of the Greek mythological character, Perseus. Although Mount Andromeda is situated next to the Columbia Icefield, the enormous cirque glacier on the mountain is self-sustaining.

The elevation and the location of the glacier on the north face of Andromeda prevent the snow from melting or evaporating, maintaining the glacier. Average annual snowfall at this elevation is seven to ten metres (23 to 33 ft). Successive snowfalls compress the previous layers into ice granules which in turn are further compressed into a solid layer of ice. The tremendous weight of this ice carves out the rock beneath it into a bowl or cirque. The weight of the glacier and the pull of gravity from below cause the ice to flow over the edge of the cirque down the mountainside. When warm air and sunlight overcome the flow rate of the ice, the glacier stops advancing.

GRAY JAY
Perisoreous canadensis

The Gray Jay is also commonly called "Whiskey Jack" from the anglicized Cree Indian name, "Wisagat chak". These friendly and appealing birds are year round residents of the southern and central Canadian Rockies and inhabit all forested areas throughout the mountains. They are usually found in pairs or small groups of four to five birds. These opportunists silently glide from tree to tree and snatch up anything that is edible. Insects, seeds, carrion and grubs are all part of the Gray Jay's natural diet. An expandable gullet permits the Gray Jay to hoard away considerable amounts of food.

The Gray Jay is often mistaken for the Clark's Nutcracker *(Nucifraga columbiana)*. Although both species are members of the Crow family and both inhabit similar mountain terrain the two birds are noticeably different. The Gray Jay is slightly smaller measuring only 28 cm (11 in) in length, with markings more subtly coloured in charcoal grey with a white face, charcoal grey crown and a light grey breast, and also tends to be quieter than the raucous Nutcracker. The Gray Jay, like the Nutcracker, is one of the earliest nesters in the Rockies, laying three to four eggs in the month of February.

MOUNT EDITH CAVELL
Jasper National Park

Located just 29 kilometres (18 mi) south of the Jasper townsite and standing 3,365 metres (11,040 ft) in elevation, Mount Edith Cavell was named to honour the daughter of Anglican minister Reverend John Cavell of Norwich, England. Edith Louisa Cavell (1865-1915) was a nurse and the Matron of the Surgical Institute of Brussels. During the outbreak of the First World War, she tended many Allied soldiers as well as German wounded. As Brussels fell to the advancing Germans, this "angel of mercy" refused to leave her post, choosing instead to continue to care for those in her charge.

On August 15, 1915, Nurse Edith Cavell was arrested by the Germans and charged with assisting English, Belgian and French soldiers to escape and return to their divisions. She was tried and blatantly admitted to the charges. At 2:00 a.m. on October 12, 1915 she was executed, despite attempts to obtain mitigation of her sentence by American Ambassador Bradley Whitlock. Edith Cavell became an inspiration and symbol of courage and dedication to the British people. A memorial service is held annually on the Sunday nearest the date of her arrest at the Anglican Church of St. Mary's and St. George in the town of Jasper.

BLACK BEAR
Ursus americanus

Black Bears are solitary animals that can be found throughout the Canadian Rockies at all elevations below the timberline, 2,450 metres (8,000 ft). All bears possess excellent hearing and an incredibly keen sense of smell that is often used to find their next meal. These omnivores have been known to travel as far as 150 km (90 mi) in order to find seasonal food sources such as roots, beargrass, dandelion and berry patches or migrating salmon. Their summertime existence is solely spent consuming food to build up body fat. Males can weigh up to 227 kg (500 lbs), females weigh on average 91 kg (200 lbs).

After mating in the summer, females (sows) have "delayed implantation". The embryo only develops if the sow is healthy and has put on enough fat reserves to see herself and her cubs through the winter. Two or three cubs weighing about 300 g (10 oz) each are born in January or February, during "estivation". This is a slowed metabolic state that is not true hibernation as once thought, since bears are known to awaken temporarily during warm spells. The cubs stay with the sow for two years, learning where and when the best food sources are available and den with her during their first winter. They may live to be 20 to 30 years old.

CALYPSO ORCHID
Calypso bulbosa

Also known as the "Venus Slipper" and the "Fairy Slipper", the Calypso Orchid is the most colourful orchid in the Canadian Rockies. This beautiful flower has five dark pink pointed sepals and petals fanning out above the lip or "slipper", which is pale pink with fine maroon marbling underneath. The top of the lip is white with bright yellow hairs. Like all orchids, the seeds need the presence of certain fungi to grow and for the plant to survive. Therefore this orchid is only found in shade on spongy moss beneath coniferous trees at lower elevations.

The Calypso Orchid grows from a small white bulb with fragile thread-like roots. Disturbing the flower tears these delicate roots and destroys the plant. The bulb produces a single dark green leaf in late August which survives through the fall and the long winter. With the arrival of spring a stem 7.5 to 15 cm (3 to 6 in) in height appears with a single bud ready to bloom in May. The captivating flower measures only 2.5 cm (1 in) in length overall. After the flower fades, the leaf withers and dies by early summer, ending the growth cycle until it begins again in late August.

61

MALIGNE LAKE
Jasper National Park

To the Stoney Indians it was known as "Chaba Imne", Beaver Lake. In 1908, using a map drawn by a Stoney Indian named Samson Beaver, Mary Schäffer (1861-1939), member of the Academy of Natural Sciences of Philadelphia and of the Geographical Society of America, along with teacher and geologist Mollie Adams, botanist Stewardson Brown, camp cook Reggie Holmes and their two guides Sidney Unwin and Billy Warren, found Maligne Lake. Exploring the lake on a raft which the men had built for the occasion, the group named the surrounding peaks and features, Mounts Unwin, Warren, Mary Vaux, Samson Peak and Samson Narrows.

The term maligne is French for "wicked" and was used by Father Pierre Jean de Smet (1801-1873), a Belgian Jesuit missionary, to describe the treacherous river that flows from the lake. The name soon spread to the lake, canyon, pass, mountain and range. At 22 kilometres (14 mi) in length it is the largest totally glacier-fed lake in North America. Spirit Island at the Samson Narrows is one of the most magnificent scenes in the Canadian Rockies and has kindled the spirit of artists, photographers and writers from around the globe. The pristine waters of Maligne Lake are located 48 kilometres (29 mi) southeast of the town of Jasper.

GREAT BLUE HERON
Ardea herodias

The Great Blue Heron is the largest heron in North America. It stands over one metre (3 ft 3 in) in height, with a wing span measuring over 1.8 metres (6 ft). This majestic bird is only a summer resident of the Rocky Mountains and spends the winter months as far south as northern South America. It can be commonly seen fishing along the edges of our mountain lakes and rivers. The Heron stands motionless, patiently waiting to spear its prey when within range of its long, sharply pointed bill. Its diet consists mainly of fish and frogs but it will also eat snakes, mice and large insects.

Unlike other herons and cranes that fly with their neck outstretched, the Great Blue Heron flies with its neck pulled back resting on its shoulders in an "S" shape and its long legs straight out behind it. During the breeding season the Heron sports two long wispy feathers from its head and long slender plumes from its lower neck and back. At this time groups of herons called heronries are established. The birds mate and nest together, building large, flat nests on the highest treetops to be used over again, year after year, with two to six eggs being laid by each pair.

OVERLANDER FALLS
Mount Robson Provincial Park

In the spring of 1862, a daring group of men led by Thomas McMicking (1827-1866), a school teacher from Queenston, travelled from Ontario in search of the newly discovered gold fields of the Cariboos in central British Columbia. The name "Overlanders" was certainly fitting as the usual route was by sea around the southern tip of South America. The courageous group arrived at Fort Garry (Winnipeg, Manitoba) in early June where they were joined by other adventurers willing to take part in the long and arduous journey westward. It was here that the only woman of the group, Catherine O'Hare Schubert, her husband Augustus and their three children joined the expedition.

The group of 175 men, one woman and three children passed Overlander Falls in late August 1862 en route to Tête Jaune Cache. Here they regrouped, rested and then headed onwards. One group went by land and water, along the North Thompson River Valley on to Fort Kamloops and the other along the Fraser River to Quesnel. Meeting a group of miners and hearing of the many hardships of the gold fields, some of the Overlanders settled in Fort Kamloops, many travelled on to the coast in search of work and others went back home. Several members of the group died during the prolonged and treacherous passage. Few actually made it to the gold fields of the Cariboos.

LEAST CHIPMUNK

Eutamias minimus

The Least Chipmunk, measuring only 8.75 to 11.25 cm (3.5 to 4.5 in) in length with a 5 cm (2 in) tail and weighing a mere 45 g (1.5 oz), is the smallest chipmunk in North America. They can be found throughout the Canadian Rockies living at all elevations. Sharing the same mountain habitat, the Golden Mantle Ground Squirrel is often mistaken for the Least Chipmunk. Although both species are members of the Rodent family the two are noticeably different. The Chipmunk is only half the size of the Golden Mantle Ground Squirrel and has black and white stripes running from the nose to the tail. Golden Mantle Ground Squirrels only have stripes from the shoulder to the tail.

As their diet consists mainly of seeds, chipmunks spend most of their time foraging on the ground but will occasionally climb coniferous trees in search of food. With the first frost they begin to gather food, filling their large cheek pouches with seeds to be carried off to an underground nest or hiding place. Chipmunks only semi-hibernate and awaken periodically to eat, relying on their food stores to survive the winter. They are in this state for approximately six months from November until April. Mating occurs in the spring after hibernation, producing a litter of three to five offspring usually in the month of June.

WESTERN WOOD LILY
Lilium philadelphicum

This strikingly vivid perennial blooms during the months of June and July and can be found growing in open deciduous woods and south-facing meadows throughout the lower montane regions of the Canadian Rocky Mountains. The floral emblem of Saskatchewan, the Western Wood Lily is also known as the "Chalice-cup Lily". It is often mistakenly called a "Tiger Lily" which is another name for the Columbia Lily *(Lilium columbianum)*. The blooms of this flower face downward as opposed to the Western Wood Lily whose flower faces upward. The true Tiger Lily *(Lilium tigrinum)* is found only in Asia.

The Western Wood Lily grows from a rough thick bulb which produces one stem 30 to 60 cm (12 to 24 in) in height. There are many narrow lance-shaped leaves along the entire length of the stem. The stem is topped by a 12.5 cm (5 in) "chalice-like" flower with three sepals and three petals which are orange turning yellow at the base with black spots, encompassing six dark stamens and one style. The plant often produces more than one bloom; three are common and occasionally five blooms per stem can be found. Due to overpicking the Western Wood Lily has protected status throughout Canada.

MOUNT ROBSON
Mount Robson Provincial Park

To the Indians it was known as "Yuh-Lai-Has-Kun", the Mountain of the Spiral Road. There are no official records on file as to whom Mount Robson was named for. However as early as 1863 the mountain was known as "Robson's Peak", probably corrupted from "Robertson". Colin Robertson (1783-1842) was an official with the Hudson's Bay Company in the 1820's and later became a member of Parliament. While with the Hudson's Bay Company, Robertson sent Iroquois fur hunters and trappers into the area. The mountain may have been named to honour John Robson, the Premier of British Columbia from 1889 to 1892, although its name preceded his term in office.

The "Monarch of the Canadian Rockies", standing at 3,954 metres (12,972 ft) in elevation, is the highest peak in the Canadian Rocky Mountains. Located 85 kilometres (54 mi) west of the Jasper townsite, it towers over the western entrance to Mount Robson Provincial Park, established as British Columbia's second provincial park on March 1, 1913. On July 31 of the same year, Conrad Kain (1883-1934), Albert Henry MacCarthy (1876-1955) and Col. William Washborough Foster (1875-1954) made the first official ascent of Mount Robson. They climbed the northeast face, now known as the Kain Face and descended by the south face to Kinney Lake.

MOOSE
Alces alces

Ranging from valley floor to timberline the Moose is the largest member of the deer family. The name is an Algonquin Indian word meaning "twig-eater", fitting since their diet consists mainly of leaves and twigs. They are easily identified by their humped shoulders, long nose and a long flap of skin hanging under the chin called a bell. Their legs are long with large flat hooves, ideally suited to swimming and diving for aquatic plants which supplement their regular diet. Throughout the summer these magnificent animals are often seen wading through marshlands and streams in search of food.

Males (bulls) may reach a shoulder height of 1.8 metres (6 ft) and weigh from 365 to 500 kg (800 to 1,100 lbs), with a massive rack measuring up to 1.8 metres (6 ft) in width and weighing 20 kg (44 lbs). As with all members of the deer family, the racks are shed in early spring. By the end of August the new set has completely regrown, ready to have the velvet rubbed off. The rut is from September to November, when the normally shy bulls become dangerously aggressive. Cows mate yearly from two years of age onwards giving birth to one calf, or occasionally to twins, in May or June. Moose can live to be 20 years old.

PYRAMID MOUNTAIN
Jasper National Park

Pyramid Mountain was known as "Priest's Rock" until 1859, when Sir James Hector (1834-1907), surgeon and geologist for the Palliser Expedition (1857-1860), named it while on an expedition to the Athabasca Pass. Its resemblance to a pyramid was noted by English adventurer Dr. Walter Butler Cheadle (1835-1910), who travelled across Canada during 1862 and 1863. Lying beneath Pyramid Mountain is Patricia Lake, named in 1914 after Princess Patricia (1886-1974), the daughter of Arthur William Patrick Albert, the Duke of Connaught and Governor General of Canada from 1911 to 1916.

Standing at an elevation of 2,766 metres (9,075 ft) and located only nine kilometres (5.5 mi) northwest of the Jasper townsite, Pyramid Mountain is one of the most prominent landmarks in the area. The mountain consists of Gog quartzite sandstone, first studied near Gog Lake in Mount Assiniboine Provincial Park in British Columbia. Gog quartzite sandstone occurs in thick layers and is unique to the Rocky Mountains due to its hardness, as other sandstone is soft, porous and grainy when broken. The red and orange colour of the rock is caused from iron oxide found in the quartzite.

ABOUT THE PHOTOGRAPHER

Bela brings an artistic precision to the subjects of his photography. Through his lenses, he is able to capture the dramatic, the aesthetic, the symmetry and texture of an object or scene, enhanced with his own perceptive perspective of the effect to be achieved. His attention to detail in both composition and technique proved to be an award-winning combination which has earned him respect throughout Canada and the United States. In 1988 at twenty-seven years of age Bela was awarded Canada's highest photographic honour, the Master of Photographic Arts Award for proven photographic quality and ability. He is the youngest recipient of the MPA Award on record.

Bela resides in Canmore, Alberta, where he enthusiastically meets the challenges of photography in the rugged wilderness of the Canadian Rockies. The results of his photographic efforts are not easily come by. Hiking, climbing, snowshoeing or skiing, Bela patiently searches out his subjects to capture them on film in their natural environment. He can be found with camera and tripod in hand scrambling over boulders after a pika, warily tracking a bear, or knee-deep in an alpine bog recording the beauty of a paintbrush. His exhilaration after being in the back country conveys his naturalist's love for the mountain wilderness and his dedication to his profession.

Nikon

Bela creates his award winning photographs which appear in his internationally best selling books and calendars using Nikon F5 and Nikon F3 cameras and Nikkor lenses exclusively. When on assignment in the rugged North American wilderness, the harsh and unforgiving Canadian Arctic or wilds of the Alaskan frontier, Nikon professional photographic equipment meets the demanding needs of Bela's photography. The combination of strong reliable construction plus leading edge technology has made Nikon Bela's only choice in 35mm photographic equipment. For more information about Nikon cameras, Nikkor lenses and accessories, visit the Nikon website at www.nikon.ca or e-mail info@nikon.ca.

We would like to thank Mary C. Mulder, National Sales, Advertising and Communications Manager, Consumer Products Division, and Nikon Canada Inc for continuing their gracious assistance and technical support throughout Bela's professional career.

When Bela needs film, gear or professional supplies, he chooses Vistek, Canada's number one choice coast to coast for photo, video and digital imaging equipment. We would like to thank Ron Silverstein, President, Vistek Ltd, for his continuing friendship and generous support since 1982. We can always depend on the professional advice and service from Vistek's knowledgeable and courteous staff.

For more information about Vistek Ltd, visit their website at: www.vistek.net. Or in Toronto, call 1-800-561-1777, and in Calgary, call 1-800-561-0333.